The Wit and Wisdom of

Ellen DeGeneres

John Jennings

For Eros

Ellen Lee DeGeneres (born January 26, 1958) is an American comedian, television host, actress, writer, and television producer. She was the star in the popular sitcom Ellen from 1994 to 1998, and has hosted her syndicated talk show The Ellen DeGeneres Show since 2003.

"Accept who you are. Unless you're a serial killer."

— Ellen DeGeneres, Seriously... I'm Kidding

"My grandmother started walking five miles a day when she was sixty. She's ninety-seven now, and we don't know where the heck she is."

— Ellen DeGeneres

"You know, it's hard work to write a book. I can't tell you how many times I really get going on an idea, then my quill breaks. Or I spill ink all over my writing tunic."

— Ellen DeGeneres, The Funny Thing Is...

"I ask people why they have deer heads on their walls. They always say because it's such a beautiful animal. There you go. I think my mother is attractive, but I have photographs of her."

— Ellen DeGeneres

"If you want to test cosmetics, why do it on some poor animal who hasn't done anything? They should use prisoners who have been convicted of murder or rape instead. So, rather than seeing if perfume irritates a bunny rabbit's eyes, they should throw it in Charles Manson's eyes and ask him if it hurts."

— Ellen DeGeneres, My Point... And I Do Have One

"Procrastinate now, don't put it off."

— Ellen DeGeneres

"Have you ever heard somebody sing some lyrics that you've never sung before, and you realize you've never sung the right words in that song? You hear them and all of a sudden you say to yourself, 'Life in the Fast Lane?' That's what they're saying right there? You think, 'why have I been singing 'wipe in the vaseline?' how many people have heard me sing 'wipe in the vaseline?' I am an idiot."

— Ellen DeGeneres, My Point... And I Do Have One

"The only thing that scares me more than space aliens is the idea that there aren't any space aliens. We can't be the best that creation has to offer. I pray we're not all there is. If so, we're in big trouble."

— Ellen DeGeneres

"In the beginning there was nothing. God said, 'Let there be light!' And there was light. There was still nothing, but you could see it a whole lot better. "

— Ellen DeGeneres

"Sometimes you can't see yourself clearly until you see yourself through the eyes of others."

— Ellen DeGeneres

"Our attention span is shot. We've all got Attention Deficit Disorder or ADD or OCD or one of these disorders with three letters because we don't have the time or patience to pronounce the entire disorder. That should be a disorder right there, TBD - Too Busy Disorder."

— Ellen DeGeneres

"Beauty is about being comfortable in your own skin. It's about knowing and accepting who you are."

— Ellen DeGeneres, Seriously... I'm Kidding

"You should never assume. You know what happens when you assume. You make an ass out of you and me because that's how it's spelled."

— Ellen DeGeneres

"Laugh. Laugh as much as you can. Laugh until you cry. Cry until you laugh. Keep doing it even if people are passing you on the street saying, "I can't tell if that person is laughing or crying, but either way they seem crazy, let's walk faster." Emote. It's okay. It shows you are thinking and feeling."

— Ellen DeGeneres, Seriously... I'm Kidding

"When you take risks you learn that there will be times when you succeed and there will be times when you fail, and both are equally important."

— Ellen DeGeneres, Seriously... I'm Kidding

"I'm a godmother, that's a great thing to be, a godmother. She calls me god for short, that's cute, I taught her that."

— Ellen DeGeneres

"Life is short. If you doubt me, ask a butterfly. Their average life span is a mere five to fourteen days."

— Ellen DeGeneres, The Funny Thing Is...

"My point is, life is about balance. The good and the bad. The highs and the lows. The pina and the colada."

— Ellen DeGeneres, Seriously... I'm Kidding

"Normal is getting dressed in clothes that you buy for work and driving through traffic in a car that you are still paying for - in order to get to the job you need to pay for the clothes and the car, and the house you leave vacant all day so you can afford to live in it."

— Ellen DeGeneres

"Procrastination is not the problem. It is the solution. It is the universe's way of saying stop, slow down, you move too fast. Listen to the music. Whoa whoa, listen to the music. Because music makes the people come together, it makes the bourgeois and the rebel. So come on people now, smile on your brother, everybody try to love one another. Because what the world needs now is love, sweet love. And I know that love is a battlefield, but boogie on reggae woman because you're gonna make it after all. So celebrate good times, come on. I've gotta stop I've gotta come to my senses, I've been out riding fences for so long... oops I did it again... um... What I'm trying to say is, if you leave tonight and you don't remember anything else

27

that I've said, leave here and remember this: Procrastinate now, don't put it off. "

— Ellen DeGeneres

"I don't need a baby growing inside me for nine months. If I'm going to feel nauseous and achy when I wake up, I want to achieve that state the old-fashioned way: getting good and drunk the night before."

— Ellen DeGeneres

"People always ask me, 'Were you funny as a child?' Well, no, I was an accountant. "

— Ellen DeGeneres

"Stuffed deer heads on walls are bad enough, but it's worse when you see them wearing dark glasses, having streamers around their necks and a hat on their antlers. Because then you know they were enjoying themselves at a party when they were shot."

— Ellen DeGeneres

"Do things that make you happy within the confines of the legal system."

— Ellen DeGeneres, Seriously... I'm Kidding

"Find out who you are and figure out what you believe in. Even if it's different from what your neighbors believe in and different from what your parents believe in. Stay true to yourself. Have your own opinion. Don't worry about what people say about you or think about you. Let the naysayers nay. They will eventually grow tired of naying."

— Ellen DeGeneres, Seriously... I'm Kidding

"What's not so great is that all this technology is destroying our social skills. Not only have we given up on writing letters to each other, we barely even talk to each other. People have become so accustomed to texting that they're actually startled when the phone rings. It's like we suddenly all have Batphones. If it rings, there must be danger.

Now we answer, "What happened? Is someone tied up in the old sawmill?"

"No, it's Becky. I just called to say hi."

"Well you scared me half to death. You can't just pick up the phone and try to talk to me like that. Don't the tips of your fingers work?"

— Ellen DeGeneres, Seriously... I'm Kidding

"True beauty is not related to what color your hair is or what color your eyes are. True beauty is about who you are as a human being, your principles, your moral compass."

— Ellen DeGeneres, Seriously... I'm Kidding

"I really don't think I need buns of steel. I'd be happy with buns of cinnamon."

— Ellen DeGeneres

"Follow your passion. Stay true to yourself. Never follow someone else's path unless you're in the woods and you're lost and you see a path. By all means, you should follow that."

— Ellen DeGeneres

"I'm so unfamiliar with the gym, I call it James!"

— Ellen DeGeneres

"If we're destroying our trees and destroying our environment and hurting animals and hurting one another and all that stuff, there's got to be a very powerful energy to fight that. I think we need more love in the world. We need more kindness, more compassion, more joy, more laughter. I definitely want to contribute to that."

- Ellen DeGeneres

"We focus so much on our differences, and that is creating, I think, a lot of chaos and negativity and bullying in the world. And I think if everybody focused on what we all have in common - which is - we all want to be happy."

- Ellen DeGeneres

"I don't pay attention to the number of birthdays. It's weird when I say I'm 53. It just is crazy that I'm 53. I think I'm very immature. I feel like a kid. That's why my back goes out all the time, because I completely forget I can't do certain things anymore - like doing the plank for 10 minutes."

- Ellen DeGeneres

"Here are the values that I stand for: honesty, equality, kindness, compassion, treating people the way you want to be treated and helping those in need. To me, those are traditional values."

- Ellen DeGeneres

"So many people prefer to live in drama because it's comfortable. It's like someone staying in a bad marriage or relationship - it's actually easier to stay because they know what to expect every day, versus leaving and not knowing what to expect."

- Ellen DeGeneres

"Find out who you are and be that person. That's what your soul was put on this Earth to be. Find that truth, live that truth and everything else will come."

- Ellen DeGeneres

"Most comedy is based on getting a laugh at somebody else's expense. And I find that that's just a form of bullying in a major way. So I want to be an example that you can be funny and be kind, and make people laugh without hurting somebody else's feelings."

- Ellen DeGeneres

"I had everything I'd hoped for, but I wasn't being myself. So I decided to be honest about who I was. It was strange: The people who loved me for being funny suddenly didn't like me for being... me."

- Ellen DeGeneres

"It's our challenges and obstacles that give us layers of depth and make us interesting. Are they fun when they happen? No. But they are what make us unique. And that's what I know for sure... I think."

- Ellen DeGeneres

"I work really hard at trying to see the big picture and not getting stuck in ego. I believe we're all put on this planet for a purpose, and we all have a different purpose... When you connect with that love and that compassion, that's when everything unfolds."

- Ellen DeGeneres

"I'm not an activist; I don't look for controversy. I'm not a political person, but I'm a person with compassion. I care passionately about equal rights. I care about human rights. I care about animal rights."

- Ellen DeGeneres

"We have two dogs, Mabel and Wolf, and three cats at home, Charlie, George and Chairman. We have two cats on our farm, Tom and Little Sister, two horses, and two mini horses, Hannah and Tricky. We also have two cows, Holy and Madonna. And those are only the animals we let sleep in our bed."

- Ellen DeGeneres

"I was raised in an atmosphere of 'everything's fine.' But as I got older, I was like, 'Well no, everything's not fine. There is stuff that's sad.' I am a really sensitive person. I think I am too sensitive sometimes."

- Ellen DeGeneres

"I like being busy and juggling a lot of things at the same time. I get bored easily, so I need to do a lot."

- Ellen DeGeneres

"I am saddened by how people treat one another and how we are so shut off from one another and how we judge one another, when the truth is, we are all one connected thing. We are all from the same exact molecules."

- Ellen DeGeneres

"I get those fleeting, beautiful moments of inner peace and stillness - and then the other 23 hours and 45 minutes of the day, I'm a human trying to make it through in this world."

- Ellen DeGeneres

"I hate having to do small talk. I'd rather talk about deep subjects. I'd rather talk about meditation, or the world, or the trees or animals, than small, inane, you know, banter."

- Ellen DeGeneres

"I'd like to be more patient! I just want everything now. I've tried to meditate, but it's really hard for me to stay still. I'd like to try to force myself to do it, because everybody says how wonderful meditation is for you, but I can't shut my mind up. So patience and learning is the key."

- Ellen DeGeneres

"The world is full of a lot of fear and a lot of negativity, and a lot of judgment. I just think people need to start shifting into joy and happiness. As corny as it sounds, we need to make a shift."

"My dad is still Christian Scientist. My mom's not, and I'm not. But I believe in God, and that there's a higher power and an intelligence that's bigger than us and that we can rely on. It's not just us, thinking we are the ones in control of everything. That idea gives me support."

- Ellen DeGeneres

"It makes a big difference in your life when you stay positive."

— Ellen DeGeneres, Seriously... I'm Kidding

"Start thinking positively. You will notice a difference. Instead of 'I think I'm a loser,' try 'I definitely am a loser.' Stop being wishy-washy about things! How much more of a loser can you be if you don't even know you are one? Either you are a loser or you are not. Which is it, stupid?"

— Ellen DeGeneres, The Funny Thing Is...

"It's failure that gives you the proper perspective on success."

— Ellen DeGeneres, Seriously... I'm Kidding

"Take a nap in a fireplace and you'll sleep like a log."

— Ellen DeGeneres

"Leaning forward in your chair when someone is trying to squeeze behind you isn't enough. You also have to move the chair."

— Ellen DeGeneres, Seriously... I'm Kidding

"I personally like being unique. I like being my own person with my own style and my own opinions and my own toothbrush."

— Ellen DeGeneres, Seriously... I'm Kidding

"When life gives you lemons....they could really be oranges."

— Ellen DeGeneres

"Our flaws are what makes us human. If we can accept them as part of who we are, they really don't even have to be an issue."

— Ellen DeGeneres, Seriously... I'm Kidding

"I wonder what will happen if I put a hand cream on my feet, will they get confused and start clapping?"

— Ellen DeGeneres, Seriously... I'm Kidding

"My life is perfect even when it's not."

— Ellen DeGeneres

"And now I've got to explain the smell that was in there before I went in there. Does that ever happen to you? It's not your fault. You've held your breath, you just wanna get out, and now you open the door and you have to explain, 'Oh! Listen, there's an odor in there and I didn't do it. It's bad."

— Ellen DeGeneres, My Point... And I Do Have One

"One time I actually cleaned out my closet so good I ended up on the cover of Time magazine."

— Ellen DeGeneres

"Who's to say what's better or worse anyway? Who's to even say what's normal or average? We're all different people and we're allowed to be different from one another. If someone ever says you're weird, say thank you. And then curtsy. No, don't curtsy. That might be too weird. Bow. And tip your imaginary hate. That'll show them."

— Ellen DeGeneres, Seriously... I'm Kidding

"Way, way back in the day, like in the 1990s, if you wanted to tell everyone you ate waffles for breakfast, you couldn't just go on the Internet and tweet it out. There was only one way to do it. You had to go outside and scream at the top of your lungs, 'I ate waffles for breakfast!' That's why so many people ended up in institutions. They seemed crazy, but when you think about it, they were just ahead of their time."

— Ellen DeGeneres, Seriously... I'm Kidding

"The thing everyone should realize is that the key to happiness is being happy for yourself and yourself."

— Ellen DeGeneres, Seriously... I'm Kidding

"Baloney is just salami with an inferiority complex."

— Ellen DeGeneres

"Things will get easier, people's minds will change, and you should be alive to see it."

— Ellen DeGeneres

"So be who you really are. Embrace who you are. Literally. Hug yourself. Accept who you are. Unless you're a serial killer."

— Ellen DeGeneres, Seriously... I'm Kidding

"The problem with labels is that they lead to stereotypes and stereotypes lead to generalizations and generalizations lead to assumptions and assumptions lead back to stereotypes. It's a vicious cycle, and after you go around and around a bunch of times you end up believing that all vegans only eat cabbage and all gay people love musicals."

— Ellen DeGeneres

"Now, I'm no scientist, but I know what endorphins are. They're tiny little magical elves that swim through your blood stream and tell funny jokes to each other. When they reach your brain, you hear what they're saying and that boosts your health and happiness. "Knock Knock... Who's There? Little endorphin... Little endorphin who? Little Endorphin Annie." And then the endorphins laugh and then you laugh. See? It's Science."

— Ellen DeGeneres, Seriously... I'm Kidding

"Haiku sounds like I'm

Saying hi to someone named

Ku. Hi, Ku. Hello."

— Ellen DeGeneres, Seriously... I'm
Kidding

"Contribute to the world. Help people. Help one person. Help someone cross the street today. Help someone with directions unless you have a terrible sense of direction. Help someone who is trying to help you. Just help. Make an impact. Show someone you care. Say yes instead of no. Say something nice. Smile. Make eye contact. Hug. Kiss. Get naked."

— Ellen DeGeneres, Seriously... I'm Kidding

"Answers to Frequently Asked Questions:

Yes.

Yes.

No.

One time in high school.

Three times in my twenties.

Rocks no salt.

Yes.

Four.

Never. And how dare you!

I will take no further questions."

— Ellen DeGeneres, Seriously... I'm Kidding

"You just have to keep driving down the road. It's going to bend and curve and you'll speed up and slow down, but the road keeps going."

— Ellen DeGeneres, Seriously... I'm Kidding

"If we don't want to define ourselves by things as superficial as our appearances, we're stuck with the revolting alternative of being judged by our actions."

— Ellen DeGeneres

"I was raised very, very strictly with Christian Science. I didn't have a shot or an aspirin or anything until I was 13 years old. We had to go to church, do testimonies every Wednesday night. I think all religion is based on what happens after this life. You live a certain way so that when you die, things can be good. But why can't things be good now? Why can't you understand that you're in heaven now? That's how I live. I believe in God. I think that God is everywhere. Every morning I look outside, and I say, "Hi, God." Because I think that the trees are God. I think that our whole experience is God."

— Ellen DeGeneres

"It always helps to think about other people instead of ourselves."

— Ellen DeGeneres, Seriously... I'm Kidding

"You know, it's hard work to write a book. I can't tell you how many times I really get going on an idea, then my quill breaks. Or I spill ink all over my writing tunic. No wonder I drink so much! Then I get so drunk, I can barely feed the baby.

That's what I call myself when I'm drunk, "The Baby."

— Ellen DeGeneres, The Funny Thing Is...

"Haters are my motivators"

— Ellen DeGeneres

"Life is about balance. The good and the bad. The highs and the lows. The thing everyone should realize is that the key to happiness is being happy by yourself and for yourself. Happiness comes from within. You have the power to change your own mindset so that all the negative, horrible thoughts that try to invade your psyche are replaced with happy, positive, wonderful thoughts."

— Ellen DeGeneres, Seriously... I'm Kidding

"Above all things physical, it is more important to be beautiful on the inside - to have a big heart and an open mind and a spectacular spleen."

— Ellen DeGeneres, Seriously... I'm Kidding

"If your Birthday is on Christmas day and you're not Jesus, you should start telling people your birthday is on June 9 or something. Just read up on the traits of a Gemini. Suddenly you're a multitasker who loves the color yellow. Because not only do you get stuck with them combo gift, you get the combo song. "We wish you a merry Christmas - and happy birthday, Terry - we wish you a merry Christmas - happy birthday, Terry - we wish you a merry Christmas and a happy New Ye - Birthday, Terry!"

— Ellen DeGeneres, Seriously... I'm Kidding

"I'm just saying we can all work on our manners. We can say please and thank you. We can be punctual. We can just be nicer to one another. It's something we have in our power to do. It reminds me of that Margaret Mead quote: "Never doubt that a small group of thoughtful, committed citizens can change the world. Indeed, it's the only thing that ever has."

— Ellen DeGeneres, Seriously... I'm Kidding

"I hope I make people feel better. I hope I take people out of their situations a little bit and make them happier. That's really why I do what I do."

— Ellen DeGeneres

"Why is it that when you wipe up dust it's called dusting but when you wipe up a spill it's not called spilling? Just something to think about."

— Ellen DeGeneres

"I cannot believe they haven't yet come up with a better screening process than the mammogram. If a man had to put his special parts inside a clamp to test him for anything, I think they would come up with a new plan before the doctor finished saying, "Put that thing there so I can crush it."

— Ellen DeGeneres, Seriously... I'm Kidding

"To be honest, I'd be the last person who should be doling out gardening advice. I don't have the patience for growing things. Yes, I realize there's nothing quite as satisfying as eating food that you've pulled up from the ground and that's why, at the height of the planting season, I bury cans of tomato soup in my backyard and dig them up in late spring."

— Ellen DeGeneres, The Funny Thing Is...

"I prefer to believe that people are good and honest and respect me enough to tell me the truth. It's not easy to find those people all the time, but they're out there."

— Ellen DeGeneres, Seriously... I'm Kidding

"It's funny how cucumber water can taste so much better than pickle juice, even though they come from the same source."

— Ellen DeGeneres, Seriously... I'm Kidding

"Be kind to one another. Bye, bye."

— Ellen DeGeneres

"When I look back on the stuff I used to wear, I wonder why somebody didn't try to stop me. Just a friendly warning, "You may regret this," would have been fine."

— Ellen DeGeneres, The Funny Thing Is...

"Quick decision makers are often stuck behind annoying people in line at Starbucks."

— Ellen DeGeneres, Seriously... I'm Kidding

"I was raised around heterosexuals, as all heterosexuals are, that's where us gay people come from... you heterosexuals."

— Ellen DeGeneres

"Do you feel insecure because you keep getting the nagging feeling that you're not that smart? Well, I've got good news for you, my friend. You have no need to be insecure. That nagging feeling is absolutely right on target. You are not that smart. But I have more good news for you. You are also not alone."

— Ellen DeGeneres, The Funny Thing Is...

"Some people believe that to find happiness, you should live each day of your life as if it's your last because that way you will appreciate every single moment you have. Other people believe that you should live each day as if it's your first because then every day can be the beginning of a new journey."

— Ellen DeGeneres, Seriously... I'm Kidding

"I think there's too much multi-tasking going on. I think people need to quiet down and focus and be still more."

— Ellen DeGeneres

"The word "yoga" literally means "uniting", because when you're doing it you are uniting your mind and your body. You can tell this almost immediately because your mind will be thinking, "Ouch, that hurts," and your body will say, "I know." And your mind will think, "You have to get out of this position." And your body will say, "I agree with you, but I can't right now. I think I'm stuck."

— Ellen DeGeneres, Seriously... I'm Kidding

"The only way a no-legged leopard could hurt you is if it fell out of a tree onto your head."

— Ellen DeGeneres, My Point... And I Do Have One

"I still get scared at night. Every tiny creak, every little noise, I open my eyes real wide and listen with them. Have you noticed that? When it's dark and you can't see a thing, you open your eyes really wide and glance back and force, like your eyes become your ears?"

— Ellen DeGeneres, My Point... And I Do Have One

"It must be around forty, when you're "over the hill." I don't even know what that means and why it's a bad thing. When I go hiking and I get over the hill, that means I'm past the hard part and there's a snack in my future. That's a good thing as far as I'm concerned."

— Ellen DeGeneres, Seriously... I'm Kidding

"Do you live each day as if it's your first or your last? Either way you should probably have a diaper on."

— Ellen DeGeneres, Seriously... I'm Kidding

"Sometimes the greatest things are the most embarrassing."

— Ellen DeGeneres, Seriously... I'm Kidding

"That's what life is all about. There's a lot of crying. So you'd better cry now and get used to it."

— Ellen DeGeneres, My Point... And I Do Have One

"There are all sorts of books offering advice on how to deal with life-threatening situations, but where's the advice on dealing with embarrassing ones?"

— Ellen DeGeneres, The Funny Thing Is...

"I enjoy growing older and wiser and learning from my mistakes every single day."

— Ellen DeGeneres, Seriously... I'm Kidding

"You're never too old to play. You're only too old for low-rise jeans."

— Ellen DeGeneres, Seriously... I'm Kidding

"True beauty is about who you are as a human being, your principles, your moral compass."

— Ellen DeGeneres, Seriously... I'm Kidding

"So let that be a lesson, kids who get an F in math. Ellen says you're doing the right thing. You're welcome, parents."

— Ellen DeGeneres, Seriously... I'm Kidding

"If we lived each day as our last, I bet we'd all be a lot more honest with people, because we wouldn't have to care what people think anymore."

— Ellen DeGeneres, Seriously... I'm Kidding

"The world is filled with negativity. I want people to watch me and think, "I feel good, and I'm going to make somebody else feel good today."

— Ellen DeGeneres

"Though you feel you're not where you're supposed to be, you shouldn't worry because that next turn that you take, it will lead you to where you want to go."

— Ellen DeGeneres

"Actually this is really funny - one time she accidentally forgot to leave a note and I had no idea she had even moved. I was living in the house with a beautiful Mexican family for three months before I realized they weren't my cousins visiting from out of town. They were so nice. They called me "Quien es, quien es," which I thought was a beautiful name."

— Ellen DeGeneres

"...we should be grateful for them because without our family—the ancestors we descend from, the cousins we see once a year, the loves our lives we see every day—life is pretty boring."

— Ellen DeGeneres, Seriously... I'm Kidding

"I like to stretch my mind by reading and writing and watching educational TV shows like The Bachelor to learn the complex mating rituals of heterosexuals."

— Ellen DeGeneres, Seriously... I'm Kidding

"There are "well-known secrets" out there and there are people who are "so happy they could die."
Sometimes people are so sad they have to laugh and sometimes things feel so wrong, they're right.
Basically what I'm saying is, I usually don't know what people are talking about."

— Ellen DeGeneres

"No one is perfect, except for Penélope Cruz."

— Ellen DeGeneres, Seriously... I'm Kidding

"What you look like on the outside is not what makes you cool... I mean, I had a mullet and I wore parachute pants for a long, long time. And I'm doing ok"

— Ellen DeGeneres

"Gratitude is looking on the brighter side of life, even if it means hurting your eyes."

— Ellen DeGeneres, The Funny Thing Is...

"Live your dreams."

— Ellen DeGeneres

"If we lived each day as our last, I bet we'd all be a lot more honest with people, because we wouldn't have to care what people think anymore. We would meet a friend for lunch and blurt out, "Hey, that's an ugly hat!" Or tell a police officer, "If you thought that was speeding, sir, you should've seen what I was doing earlier! I think that was the fastest I've ever driven." Or if you break up with someone you would finally tell them, "I just want you to know, it's not me. It's you."

— Ellen DeGeneres, Seriously... I'm Kidding

"I remember when I was probably about ten years old I had a pen pal, and writing letters back and forth with him was one of my favorite things to do. His name was Steve and he lived in one of those huge mansions that's so big it has a name. It was called the Louisiana State Penitentiary, and he told me it was even bigger than the mayor's mansion. We'd send letters back and forth and he'd ask me to send him my favorite books and small pieces of metal or wood that were lying around and all the money I could find in my house. And I'd gather them all up and put cute little stickers of cats on the packages and send them away. It was so fun. Eventually we stopped writing because I moved to another city and he moved out to live on his own. He called it "solitary confinement." I was always so impressed by his vocabulary."

— Ellen DeGeneres, Seriously... I'm Kidding

"Enjoy your life. God gave us our bodies as a gift. (Granted, to some of us it's kind of a gag gift, but that's okay too.) Wear what you want, love who you want, and have fun."

— Ellen DeGeneres, The Funny Thing Is...

"You never know what funny can do."

— Ellen DeGeneres

"Let's try and pay more attention to what's around us. Look up. Look down - if only so you don't trip. Ask questions. You know how kids always ask "why?" Ask why. Then ask why again. And then ask why again. And then ask why again. And then ask why again. And then ask why again. And then ask why again. And then ask why again. Don't stop asking why until you get the answer you're looking for. Or until you're escorted away by security, whichever comes first."

— Ellen DeGeneres, Seriously... I'm Kidding

"I personally like being unique. I like being my own person with my own style and my own opinion and my own toothbrush. I think it's so much better to stand out in some way and to set yourself apart from the masses. It would be so boring to look out into the world and see hundreds of people who look and think exactly like me. If I wanted that, I could just sit in front of a mirror and admire my own reflection all day."

— Ellen DeGeneres

"I spend a lot of time exploring my body. Hang on, that doesn't sound quite right. What I mean to say is, I like to constantly be in touch with my own body. Okay, that's not right, either. My body is a wonderland. I don't even know why I just said that."

— Ellen DeGeneres, Seriously... I'm Kidding

"Sometimes I get so lost in the moment, I start running around my yard, flapping my arms like a seagull at the beach. A lot of times I'll even start to squawk. Usually right around the third or fourth squawk is when my neighbor starts screaming at me to pipe down. He's always like, "Quiet down, lady! And put on some pants!" And I'm always like, "YOU put on some pants, sir!" because in the heat of the moment I panic and I can't think of anything better to say. Of course, he's already wearing pants, so it doesn't pack quite the punch I want it to, but the bottom line is he's clearly not as connected to nature as I am."

— Ellen DeGeneres, Seriously... I'm Kidding

"My point is, I love gardening as a hobby. Right now in our garden, Portia and I are growing tomatoes, peppers, zucchini, beets, eggplant, basil, and a whole assortment of herbs. It smells nice, it looks nice, and I can't tell you how satisfying it is to be able to host a dinner party and offer my quests the literal fruits of my labor. (As it turns out, these are very different than the fruits of one's loins. At a recent dinner party, I accidently asked Martha Stewart how she was enjoying the fruits of my loins and she nearly choked on her stew.)"

— Ellen DeGeneres, Seriously... I'm Kidding

"It's hard to understand failure when you're going through it, but in the grand scheme of things it's good to fall down—not because you're drunk and not near stairs."

— Ellen DeGeneres, Seriously... I'm Kidding

"I don't know when it became socially acceptable to be late."

— Ellen DeGeneres, Seriously... I'm Kidding

"Knowledge is power and you need power in this world. You need as many advantages as you can get."

— Ellen DeGeneres

"...there are a lot of self-righteous people out there. And if you try to adjust your life to please them...you're just going to go crazy and risk being as unhappy as these self-righteous kooks are."

— Ellen DeGeneres, The Funny Thing Is...

Made in the USA
Middletown, DE
18 December 2018